EAGLES

First published in Great Britain in 1999 by
Colin Baxter Photography Ltd
Grantown-on-Spey
Moray PH26 3NA
Scotland

WorldLife Library Series

A CIP Catalogue record for this book is available from the British Library

ISBN 1-900455-59-5

Printed in Hong Kong

Page one: Like an airplane landing with its flaps down, this golden eagle uses its wings and tail to slow its airspeed as it reaches for its perch. (Photo © W. Perry Conway)
Page four: Soaring eagles have long inspired humans to dream of worlds above. (Photo © Henry H. Holdsworth)

EAGLES

Rebecca L. Grambo

Colin Baxter Photography, Grantown-on-Spey, Scotland

Contents

Introduction   7

Origins and Definitions   9

Physical Features   11

Hunting, Diet, and Migration   19

Home and Family   27

Eagle Groups   37

Golden Eagle   47

Bald Eagle   55

Eagles and Humans   63

The Future   67

Index   70

Recommended Reading   71

Introduction

For centuries untold, humans have fallen under the eagle's spell. Cruising low over the ground, tip-tilting its wing feathers with exquisite control or climbing effortlessly into the pure blue of a spring sky until it almost disappears, the eagle has been a source of inspiration and an object of veneration for people the world over. The size and power of the eagle, as well as its soaring flight, have given it a special place as a cultural symbol. Above all, the eagle has long served as an emblem of authority, and its likeness can be found on flags, coins, and official seals around the world.

When people first adopted the eagle as a symbol, they lived their lives in daily contact with the land, and eagles were not merely abstract symbols but real animals that could be seen overhead. Today, the only contact many of us have with "eagles" is in the names of sports teams or commercial enterprises. We have retained our admiration for the symbol, but have lost our connection with the living creature that so fired the human imagination in days gone by.

Real eagles are far more impressive than corporate logos—they are awe-inspiring hunters, gentle and attentive parents, and masters of the winds. Although most of us think of only one or two different birds when we hear the word "eagle," there are more than sixty species of eagles living around the world. Many of these populations are feeling the pressure of habitat loss and degradation, and some of the most spectacular eagles are facing extinction. Learning more about eagles helps us to appreciate how much they bring to our world and to make informed decisions to ensure they will always be a part of it.

The fate of eagles is irrevocably linked to the decisions we are now making. It is our job to see that our choices are wise ones. (Photo © Henry H. Holdsworth)

Origins and Definitions

The fossil record shows that the earliest predatory birds appeared thirty to fifty million years ago. By about fifteen million years ago, raptors could be seen in the skies over much of the Old and New Worlds. There seem to be no direct links, however, between these ancient hunters and our modern birds of prey. The eagles of today are members of the family Accipitridae, the largest of the five groups of raptors that make up the order Falconiformes. The other four families in the order are the Cathartidae (New World vultures), Falconidae (falcons and caracaras), and two single species families, the Pandionidae (osprey) and Sagittaridae (secretary bird).

Renowned ornithologist Leslie Brown has defined an eagle as "a large or very large diurnal raptor which is not a kite, buzzard, vulture, hawk or falcon." In other words, eagles are large birds of prey that are active mainly during the day that cannot be placed into any of the more clearly defined categories of raptors. Defining eagles by what they are not rather than by what they are has led to some birds being called eagles by one authority and something else by another, and just how eagle species are related to one another is still unknown. Recent technological advances offer hope that this situation will change. New information from genetic testing may help to unravel tangled relationships, aid in clarifying classification, and even provide scientists with clues about the evolutionary history of the Accipitridae.

The evolutionary family tree of eagles is unclear, and so are the relationships between the various eagle species. (Photo © Michael H. Francis)

Physical Features

The word "eagle" conjures up the image of a big, powerfully built bird, and some eagles more than fit this description. The Philippine eagle (*Pithecophaga jefferyi*) may be as tall as 3 feet (1 m), possess a wingspan of nearly 6.6 feet (2 m), and weigh up to 14.3 pounds (6.5 kg). The harpy eagle (*Harpia harpyja*) is even more impressive: height about 3 feet (1 m), wingspan reaching as much as 7.5 feet (2.3 m), weight nearly 20 pounds (9 kg). At the other end of the scale, however, are eagles so small that they could be mistaken for hawks. The Nias serpent eagle (*Spilornis cheela asturinus*) has a wingspan of barely 3 feet (1 m), less than that of many hawks. The little eagle (*Hieraaetus morphnoides*) is only 16 to 19 inches (41–48 cm) tall and weighs 2 to 2.5 pounds (0.9–1.1 kg). Ayres's hawk-eagle (*Hieraaetus ayresii*) is even smaller, standing as tall as the little eagle but weighing only about 1.5 pounds (0.7 kg), making it smaller than a common crow.

In all eagle species, the females are larger than the males. The size difference is greatest in those species that are the most aggressive and that specialize in avian prey. The reason for this sexual dimorphism is unknown but a number of theories have been put forward. A larger female may be better able to defend the nest or to withstand the physical demands of incubation and chick tending. A smaller male may be more agile in the air—an important quality given that males do most of the hunting during the incubation and nestling periods.

Eagles are hunters, and their bodies are exquisitely designed for the tasks they must perform. A pair of extraordinary eyes gives the eagle its legendary vision—it is estimated that an eagle's visual acuity is at least four to eight times that of a human. In practical terms that means that a grazing rabbit may be visible to an eagle flying as far as 2 miles (3.2 km) away. As the eagle swoops down on its prey, muscles in the eagle's eyes continuously adjust the curvature of the eyeballs to maintain sharp focus and accurate depth perception throughout the attack. Eagle eyes give much better depth perception than human eyes and are far superior at distinguishing detail. Eagle eyes are also large: a 10-pound (4.5-kg) eagle may have eyes as big as those belonging to a 200-pound (90.7-kg) human. These large eyes fill their sockets to such an extent that there is little room for them to move, forcing an eagle to turn its entire head to see off to the side

The excellent vision of an eagle, four to eight times better than a human's, allows it to spy potential meals from great distances. (Photo © W. Perry Conway)

rather than just moving its eyes in their sockets as a human does.

Once the eyes have spotted a potential meal, the task of capturing and holding the prey is handled by the other end of the eagle—its talons. Capable of inflicting severe wounds, an eagle's sharp talons are incredibly strong and once clenched in flesh, exceedingly difficult to pry open. Most eagles have their four toes arranged in a similar fashion—three toes pointing forward, with the outer two slightly turned out to the side, and one toe pointing to the rear. The inward-curving, needle-sharp tips of these toes are driven towards each other by powerful tendons as the eagle strikes its prey. The victim's struggles only work the talons deeper into its body, where they fatally damage the spinal cord or vital organs.

The martial eagle is the largest African eagle. A female may have a wingspan of 8.5 feet (2.6 meters). (Photo © Jeremy Woodhouse)

Some eagles have evolved slightly modified talons to suit their specific lifestyles. The gray-headed fish eagle (*Ichthyophaga ichthyaetus*) and the lesser fish eagle (*Ichthyophaga humilis*), which dine almost exclusively on fish, have two toes facing forward and two backward. This arrangement, plus the fact that the toes have sharp, pointed scales on them, help the eagles hold on to their slippery catches. The short, powerful toes of snake eagles can grip a squirming reptile securely, and the thick scales on these eagles' legs may help to protect them from snake bites. The talons of another dietary specialist, the black eagle (*Ictinaetus malayensis*), are long and relatively straight, effectively giving it a bigger footspan. As it flies slowly over the treetops, this eagle looks for birds' nests, then snatches up eggs, nestlings, or sometimes whole nests.

Two more excellent examples of evolutionary talon specialization are the martial eagle (*Polemaetus bellicosus*) and its relative the crowned hawk-eagle (*Stephanoaetus coronatus*). The martial eagle searches the African savannas for its favorite prey—gamebirds. The eagle's long legs with large feet ending in long, slender toes are ideal for reaching out and grabbing birds as they flee. The crowned hawk-eagle does its

The golden eagle looks like what most humans imagine an "eagle" to be. (Photo © W. Perry Conway)

The finely controlled power of this golden eagle's wings allow the bird to snatch up moving prey or make pinpoint landings. (Photo © W. Perry Conway)

hunting over Africa's forests, woodlands, and rocky hills. Despite being smaller and lighter than the martial eagle, the crowned hawk-eagle's strong, short, thick toes and stout, stiff talons enable it to handle bigger game than its relative. A record exists of a crowned hawk-eagle killing a bushbuck weighing 35 pounds (15.9 kg)—four times as much as the eagle. The attacking eagle apparently landed on the bushbuck's back, held on with one foot while plunging the other set of talons into the animal's neck, and finally killed the bushbuck by asphyxiation or by piercing its spinal cord.

Once prey is subdued, strong, hooked beaks and powerful jaw muscles are used for tearing strips of flesh from a carcass. Beaks, too, have evolved to suit the foods on which they are most often employed. Snake eagles, which often swallow their prey whole, have smaller beaks than eagles like the Steller's sea eagle (*Haliaeetus pelagicus*), which requires its substantial beak for ripping open the tough skins of seal pups and fish.

To get in position to use its formidable weaponry, an eagle relies on its wings. The wings of most eagles are long and broad, providing both lift and control when soaring. The front edges of the wings are thicker than the trailing edges, causing air to flow faster over the tops of the wings, creating lift. The tapered ends of the primary feathers become widely separated at the wing tips when the eagle fully extends its wings. This reduces turbulence as air passes over the end of the wings, making for more efficient flight. Although its wings may appear motionless, a soaring eagle is constantly fine-tuning the position of its primaries in response to changes in the air flow. In addition to controlling their flight with their wings, eagles use their tail feathers to help with steering and stopping.

Just as they have evolved specialized talons and beaks, eagles living varied lifestyles possess different kinds of wings and tails. The harpy eagle lives in tropical forests from Mexico south to Argentina. Like forest-dwelling eagles in other parts of the world, it has shorter, more rounded wings and a longer tail than eagles living in open lands. This adaptation helps the harpy to maneuver through areas congested with foliage. The broad wings and short tails of fish eagles provide the powerful lift needed to pull struggling fish or birds from the water. The colorful bateleur (*Terathopius ecaudatus*) has long, narrow wings and an almost non-existent tail, making it a fast, straight-line glider. It can cruise above the African savanna at 40 to 50 miles per hour (64–80 km/h) for hours at a time, and regularly covers hundreds of miles in a day.

Attached to an eagle's powerful wings is a lightweight body frame made of hollow, air-filled bones. The

flesh that covers this frame is insulated and streamlined with another lightweight material—feathers. For an example of the relative weights involved, consider a 14-pound (6.4-kg) bald eagle (*Haliaeetus leucocephalus*): Bones account for slightly more than 4 percent of its weight; its seven thousand feathers make up approximately 9 percent.

Eagle feathers come in many shapes and serve several purposes. The small, soft down feathers insulate the eagle's body. Feathers along the bird's breast and back streamline the eagle, reducing air resistance. Tiny, single shaft feathers found near the base of the bill and around the eyes give the eagle the same kind of sensory information that whiskers give a cat. And finally, the flight feathers on an eagle's wings and tail provide the lift and control needed for precision flight.

The soft breast feathers of an eagle are made of the same substance as its stiff flight feathers, and as a human's hair and nails—keratin. (Photo © Henry H. Holdsworth)

Thanks to a combination of great power, relatively low weight, and wingtip control, eagles are some of the world's most impressive fliers, climbing high into the sky in apparently effortless spirals and swooping down onto prey in tremendous rushes of speed. When you watch an eagle in flight, you are seeing not only the bird in the sky but the product of countless years of evolution—a creature superbly adapted for the life it leads.

Caught in mid-wingbeat, this bald eagle may look awkward but that is a false impression. Eagles are some of the world's most powerful and graceful fliers. (Photo © Frank Oberle)

Hunting, Diet, and Migration

An eagle drifting across the sky may appear to be an aimless wanderer, but when it spies potential prey, the eagle's flight becomes intensely purposeful. If the target is another bird, the eagle may rocket down from its soaring height and attempt to snatch the bird in mid-air. Bonelli's eagle (*Hieraaetus fasciatus*) hunts over the rocky, wooded mountain areas of Eurasia and Africa. Reported to dive at speeds approaching 200 miles per hour (322 km/h), this eagle adds its own twist to this pursuit: It may actually go slightly past its target, then turn its talons upward to make its grab. Above the forests and woods of sub-Saharan Africa, another soaring hunter, Ayres's hawk-eagle (*Hieraaetus ayresii*), will chase its winged quarry from the sky right into the trees, jinking and weaving among the branches. If a hunting eagle catches sight of a small mammal or other prey on the ground, the bird waits until the prey is out from cover and exposed, then dives upon it. Some species, including golden eagles and wedge-tailed eagles, come in low over the ground, then drop suddenly to snatch up prey like hare or grouse.

Whether eagles are hunting birds in the air or creatures on the ground, only about one in four airborne attacks is successful. Airborne attacks use relatively large quantities of energy for uncertain gain, and not all eagles hunt this way. Many prefer to perch on a tree or telephone pole and wait. Eagles that still-hunt in this fashion must often sit for hours until a small mammal or reptile appears. They then dive rapidly from their perches onto the moving target—not an easy task. Many of the reptile-eating eagles and some of the fish-eating eagles do most of their hunting this way. The lesser spotted eagle (*Aquila pomarina*), found in eastern Europe and India, goes one step further and is an active ground-hunter. It can sometimes be seen stalking around on its relatively long legs, looking for the small rodents it likes to eat.

Fish-eating eagles have more than one method of catching their meals. The hunt may be as easy as picking up dead or dying post-spawning fish. Bald eagles and Steller's sea eagles both regularly exploit this food source. More active prey demands more forceful capture. Some eagles employ a one-foot snatch technique on fish swimming near the surface. Other eagles, once they spy a fish, plunge right into the water with both talons. Sometimes an eagle latches onto a fish or waterfowl that is too heavy for it to lift from

Most eagles live by active hunting—day in, day out. This eagle may have young in the nest, adding extra urgency to its quest for food. (Photo © Frank Oberle)

the water. Reluctant to release such a bonanza, the eagle may slowly "row" its way to shore using its wings. The bald eagle also practices aerial piracy, chasing fish-laden ospreys and forcing them to drop their catches. Although this form of piracy is most commonly observed among the fish eagles, others, such as the steppe eagle (*Aquila nipalensis*) and the tawny eagle (*Aquila rapax*), employ it as well.

Strong talons securely gripping slippery prey, a bald eagle lifts its prize from the water. (Photo © Frank Oberle)

The diet of eagles is not limited to reptiles, rodents, birds, and fish. Ornithologist Leslie Brown states that they will "eat anything, dead or alive, from termites to dead elephants and whales." Snakes, seal pups, frogs, crabs, monkeys, sloths, and assorted carrion are just some of their other preferred foods.

While eagles in general have a widely varying menu, many species have definite food preferences. Carrion plays an important role in the diet of the white-tailed sea eagle (*Haliaeetus albicilla*) and Pallas' sea eagle (*Haliaeetus leucoryphus*), particularly in winter when other food may be scarce.

The carrion may take the form of isolated bird, fish, or mammal carcasses that provide food for one, or it may take the form of a large source that draws a huge congregation of hungry eagles. Such a gathering of Steller's sea eagles occurs at Kuril Lake on Russia's Kamchatka Peninsula, which is Asia's largest sockeye salmon spawning ground. As many as one thousand of these large eagles come to feed on the salmon carcasses and eggs.

Another sea eagle, the white-bellied sea eagle (*Haliaeetus leucogaster*), has an appetite for sea snakes, which the eagle plucks from the water when they surface to breathe. The many snake and serpent eagles were given their names because of their preferred prey. Even though they eat the same type of food, snake and serpent eagles deal with their catches differently. Serpent eagles tend to fly off with the snakes dangling from their feet. Snake eagles use a more secure method of transport: they eat the snakes. After

When eagles gather, occasional squabbles may break out among the usually territorial birds. Here, a choice perch is the cause of the dispute. (Photo © Henry H. Holdsworth)

breaking the reptile's back and crushing its head, some snake eagles swallow the snake whole, headfirst. Both venomous and harmless snakes are handled in this way, and the eagles are not harmed by snake venom, which they simply digest. One explanation for this behavioral difference is that serpent eagles, in general, hunt in more forested terrain and are less vulnerable to having their meals snatched from their grasps by another raptor. The habit of swallowing prey whole makes for an interesting sight when a snake eagle parent feeds its young at the nest. The hungry eaglet grasps the bit of snake tail protruding from its parent's beak and pulls, extracting the intact snake from the adult's crop with all the panache of a magician producing a string of handkerchiefs from a volunteer's suit pocket.

Other eagles, too, have their dietary mainstays. In Africa, Verreaux's eagle (*Aquila verreauxii*) is quite capable of killing an animal as large as a small deer, but it apparently finds the rabbit-sized rock hyrax the ideal prey. This eagle prefers to nest near hyrax colonies and usually chooses other foods only if the rodents are in short supply. When alates, the winged forms of ants and termites, are swarming, steppe eagles wintering in Africa may make the insects their main food. The eagles do this even though they must gobble up huge quantities of such small prey to obtain sufficient nourishment. The lesser spotted eagle is especially fond of amphibians, which can compose as much as 42 percent of its total diet. The long-crested eagle (*Lophoaetus occipitalis*) prefers to eat mostly rats and mice, while another African species, the vulturine fish eagle (*Gypohierax angolensis*), is an oddity among the almost exclusively carnivorous eagles. It eats a variety of foods, including snails, fish, crabs, and locusts, but greatly prefers the fruit of the oil palm.

Wherever and whatever it hunts, an eagle must find enough food to satisfy its minimum energy requirements. The smaller the prey it takes, the more time the eagle must spend hunting. It is somewhat surprising, then, to learn that most eagles spend a good deal of their time resting. This is probably to conserve valuable energy, but it also relates to their dependence on the winds. Eagles that are soaring hunters must wait to take wing until the air has warmed enough to create the rising air currents or "thermals" they need—the heavier the eagle, the later in the day it begins to hunt. Heavy rain usually keeps eagles grounded, but where the climate is consistently wet, such as on the Queen Charlotte Islands of British Columbia, hungry eagles learn to cope and fly despite the weather.

Sailing in close to the ground, a golden eagle is able to surprise an unwary prairie dog. (Photo © W. Perry Conway)

The unending quest for food is also the driving force behind the annual migrations of some eagles. In warm climates, where food is usually plentiful, eagles rarely leave their homes. The exceptions are some African species, which shift location slightly during the rainy season. Game prefers to stay under cover when it is wet, and tropical rains may roil the waters of fishing grounds, making it difficult to see prey.

Bald eagles, as well as some other eagles, are aerial pirates. They will chase and harass a fish-laden osprey, or in this case, another eagle, in the hopes of snatching up a dropped catch. (Photo © Henry H. Holdsworth)

A temporary move to a drier area provides better hunting. Eagles living farther north, where winters can be severe, make their long treks to the south when their usual sources of food take cover from the elements. Better weather means more animals out moving around, and that translates into increased opportunities for a meal. Within a single species, southern populations in consistently productive hunting grounds may stay put while northern populations migrate as prey availability fluctuates. Some Florida bald eagles do things a little differently, migrating north for the summer.

Migrating eagles avoid expending excessive energy on their long-distance travels by using thermals, which are most often found over rough terrain. Spiraling to the heights on one of these natural elevators, an eagle can then glide "downhill" until it finds another updraft to lift it skyward again. Because of this dependence on thermals, migrating eagles fly only during the day and only when it is sunny and dry. The migration routes of eagles avoid large bodies of water, where thermals are scarce, and instead funnel along mountain ranges, where the birds can find the updrafts they need. Other raptors make this annual trek, too, also relying on thermals, and the sheer number of birds concentrated along the three major flyways from Europe to Africa and the Middle East is astounding. During the 1985 spring migration, for example, 1.2 million raptors of twenty-eight species were counted at Elat, Israel, near the head of the Gulf of Aquaba.

Gatherings of eagles occur when there is a large food source. When salmon spawn, the feast of dead and dying fish may attract thousands of birds. (Photo © Frank Oberle)

Home and Family

Once an eagle reaches sexual maturity, at about four to five years of age, its life becomes centered around finding a mate and raising a family. In many eagle species, mated pairs appear to remain together throughout their lives and return to the same area each year to nest. To attract the attention of a mate or to strengthen an existing pair bond, eagles may perform stunning courtship flights. Some eagles execute great pendulum sweeps, shooting downward from the sky with folded wings, then pulling out of the dive, extending their wings, and swooping upward again. Verreaux's eagles may plummet more than 1,000 feet (305 m) during these displays. In other species, a pair may be soaring together when the male suddenly dives toward the female. She rolls over as he passes and extends her feet until they almost touch the male's, then finishes her roll and drops away. The eagle pair may repeat this maneuver again and again. Some of the sea eagles have taken this display to spectacular lengths. Instead of merely touching feet, the female grips the male's feet firmly in hers and the pair cartwheel down from the sky, wings outstretched, tumbling over one another, until the two finally separate near the ground or water and climb upwards once more.

A pair of eagles selects and defends a territory, within which they hunt and raise their young. For a pair of large eagles, this area may stretch over 40 to 120 square miles (100–300 sq km). Eagles advertise their possession of a territory by making highly visible display flights or, as the African fish eagle (*Haliaeetus vocifer*) often does, by calling loudly from a prominent perch. Thanks to this means of warning off intruders, direct confrontations are rare. Eagles are most territorial during their breeding season and their protective behavior reaches its peak while they have eaglets at the nest. The harpy eagle and crowned hawk-eagle are especially aggressive around their nests and will even attack approaching humans, but a strong sense of self-preservation causes most eagles to flee if an intruder nears. This trait is the reason that one should be extremely careful not to disturb nesting eagles. They may abandon the nest, along with any eggs or chicks, if they feel threatened.

In most eagle pairs, it is apparently the female that selects the location of the nest, or aerie. She also

Some eagles are vocal communicators, and a pair may do a great deal of calling during courtship and nesting. The bald eagle's cry has been well described as sounding like a rusty hinge. (Photo © Henry H. Holdsworth)

A bald eagles surveys its domain, searching for prey with its excellent vision.
(Photo © Frank Oberle)

does most of the assembly with materials brought to her by her mate. Nests may be built in trees, on rocky ledges and cliff faces, or even on the ground. Eagles, particularly those living in temperate climates, may have more than one nest site in their territory and may alternate between locations from year to year. Most species seem to have a preferred type of nest location, but individual birds often have their own idiosyncratic preferences. For example, although golden eagles around the world usually nest on cliff faces, some golden eagles in Saskatchewan nest in trees.

The nest of an eagle can be a modest, annually constructed affair or a massive structure used and added to by several generations of birds. Snake eagles, and other smaller eagles, usually start their small, somewhat scraggly nests from scratch each year. The big eagles, such as bald eagles and white-tailed sea eagles, prefer to refurbish existing aeries, adding a fresh layer of material to the top. When this process is continued over a long period of time and the underlying supports are strong enough, the resulting nest may reach astounding proportions. When measured in 1922, a famous bald eagle nest in Vermilion, Ohio, was 12 feet (3.6 m) tall, 8.5 feet (2.6 m) across the top, and weighed an estimated 2 tons (1.8 tonnes)—more than four hundred times the weight of one of its builders. It eventually became too big for the supporting branches and collapsed.

Mouth agape, a young bald eagle sits amidst the remnants of past meals. (Photo © Scott Nielsen)

Nests are commonly constructed of sticks and branches with leaves, moss, and grass used to fill gaps; however, eagles are quite capable of substituting alternate materials for these standards. In the Aleutian Islands, bald eagles compensate for a lack of trees by building their nests on the ground with seaweed. African fish eagles sometimes use the nests of weaverbirds to plug holes in their own nests. Rope, cornstalks, and rags have all been seen built into aeries. An eagle's nest spotted in North Dakota in 1882 was built with bison rib bones. Bird-banders have made note of many strange objects in eagle nests, including light bulbs, newspapers, buttons, a candle, a framed photograph, and even a pair of pink panties. Whether these items were intended to be used as building materials, food, or even decoration is known only to the eagles.

Along with all the other nest materials, eagles frequently bring sprays of fresh greenery to the nest throughout their tenancy. The amount of material brought is greatest before incubation begins and then, as the eaglets hatch and begin to grow, the supply diminishes. No one knows for certain why eagles bring green branches to the nest, although there are several theories: Periodically relining the nest cup helps to keep the nest clean and reduces the problem of parasite infestation; the leafy branches shade the eaglets; the eagles are decorating the nest in some way. While none of these theories is completely satisfactory, observers have noted that green branches are exciting possessions for eagles. The male brings many sprigs of green to the female while they are courting, and branches are often brought when it is time for an incubation shift-change.

Nest building and associated activities are integral parts of eagle courtship. A male banded snake eagle may woo his chosen mate by bringing frogs or snakes to a favorite feeding place near the nest. Called by the male, the female flies to him and eats his offering. This ritual may occur almost daily during their courtship. Although most eagles copulate throughout their breeding season, mating is more frequent during the time the eagles are building their nests, and it often takes on an increased sense of urgency around the nest site: One amorous pair of African fish eagles was seen mating six times in one morning, and banded snake eagles have been seen mating on the ground after falling, claws locked together, from their nest tree.

The total amount of time a pair of eagles spends working on the nest can range from about a week for a quick fix-up on an existing temperate-zone nest to several months for construction of a new nest in the tropics. Eagles living in the tropics take longer to build their nests than their relatives dwelling in more variable climates, possibly because they lack the urgency imposed by an impending change of seasons. When eggs must be laid, chicks hatched, fed, and fledged—and all of this done while the good weather holds—there is little time to waste. Species nesting in the North do so as early and as quickly as possible. It is not unusual for bald eagles arriving in Canada in early spring to weather at least one snowstorm hunkered down on the nest. When the aerie finally meets with parental approval, the arrival of the first egg is not long delayed.

With freshly caught prey grasped in its talons, a bald eagle ascends to a perch to dine. (Photo © Frank Oberle)

An eagle's eggs are unremarkable in appearance, usually a speckled off-white or buff color. In most eagle species, both parents patiently share the forty-plus days of incubating their one to three eggs. The great birds carefully clench their talons into balls before settling in to brood and then position them carefully in the nest, so as not to damage eggs or chicks. When the eggs finally hatch, the newly emerged eaglets look nothing like their imposing parents. Covered in soft, whitish down, the chicks squat on wobbly legs that are too weak to support their weight. Partially closed eyes limit the eaglets' vision and their heads loll to the side, insufficiently supported by their neck muscles. These helpless eaglets must rely completely on the care and protection of their parents. The female remains nearly constantly at the nest with her new offspring. The male has the responsibility of providing enough food for his rapidly growing family. As the eaglets mature, the female begins to hunt more frequently, but initially she concentrates her energies on caring for the small creatures tucked beneath her.

It is usually the female who patiently feeds each tiny chick, gently coaxing it to take a shred of meat from her fiercely hooked beak. Over and over she offers food, eating rejected morsels herself, then tearing off a new piece to try again. Both parents use their bodies to shelter the fragile chicks from the elements, sitting stolidly on the nest through drenching rains and in baking sun. Eagle parents do their best to protect their offspring from external hazards but, for some eaglets, the greatest threat to their survival is sitting next to them in the nest.

Eagles lay their eggs several days apart, rather than all at one time. As a result, the chicks hatch at different times, and the firstborn almost always has a size advantage over its siblings. In some eagle species, the eldest uses this advantage to kill any nest mates in what is known as "Cain and Abel" behavior, or simply "Cainism." The bigger chick repeatedly pecks at the smaller chick until the injured bird dies from its injuries, or becomes too weak to solicit food from a parent and dies of starvation. At this point, the chick's corpse is usually consumed either by the surviving chick or by its parents: To the eagles, the dead chick is nothing more than food that is not allowed to go to waste.

The reasons behind Cain and Abel behavior are still unclear. It does not seem to be simply competition for food, as Cainism may occur even if there is plenty of food at the nest. Valerie Gargett, who studied Verreaux's eagles, feels that the weaker chick would just as readily kill the stronger were it physically able, and believes that it is genetically determined that in some species of eagle a chick will kill its sibling. She

The gentleness of the female eagle while feeding her chicks has mesmerized many observers. (Photo © W. Perry Conway)

adds that this behavior may have evolved when it was somehow advantageous and presently exists because it is not detrimental to species' survival. However, for eagles with declining populations, like the lesser spotted eagle, Cain and Abel behavior has become a problem. Scientists have successfully removed threatened eaglets from nests and fostered them under other birds, saving these valuable additions to the species so they can play their part in producing future generations of eagles.

Eaglets that survive the perils of the nest grow steadily larger and stronger, and their fluffy down is gradually replaced by feathers. The nest platform becomes an exercise area as the eaglets bound up and down, flapping their wings. These workouts grow more and more enthusiastic until one day the eaglets take wing for the first time. The time between hatching and first flight can range from 60 days for temperate-zone eagles like the golden eagle and short-toed snake eagle, to almost 150 days for the big, tropical forest species like the harpy eagle. First flights are more often glides than controlled flights, and landings are something else again. Inexperienced eagles may try to land with the wind behind them and end up pushed past the branch for which they were aiming. If they grab for the perch and hang on, the end result may be a confused eaglet hanging upside down from a branch like a large, ungainly bat. The young eagles learn, though, and eventually take wing with confidence and control.

The newly airborne eaglets may remain in the vicinity of the aerie for some time, sharing food caught by their parents while they hone their own hunting skills. This period of dependency may last for nearly a year in some large species, like the harpy eagle, crowned hawk-eagle, and martial eagle. Staying together this long apparently provides a longer learning period and reduces mortality during the dangerous first year of life; however, it also means that the adults of these species can breed only once every two years, lowering the reproduction rate. Eventually, young eagles leave to seek out territories of their own. If they escape the many hazards that claim approximately 70 percent of eagles and other raptors before they reach sexual maturity, these newest members of an ancient race will find mates and take their place in the unending cycle of the aerie.

Much of an eagle's life is determined by the wind and the eagle's mastery of it. (Photo © Frank Oberle)

Eagle Groups

Scientists loosely divide eagles into four groups based on their physical characteristics and behavior: sea or fish eagles, snake or serpent eagles, booted or true eagles, and harpy or buteonine eagles.

Sea or Fish Eagles

Eleven species of eagles live on the forested shores of lakes, rivers, and oceans from the Arctic Circle to the tropics, excluding South America. Their diet is heavily weighted, as one would guess from their name, in favor of fish, which may be taken alive or as carrion. However, one bird sometimes placed in this group, the vulturine fish eagle, is a near-vegetarian, dining almost exclusively on the fruit of the oil palm. (This bird is also called the palm-nut vulture; it appears to be somewhere between fish eagles and vultures in both anatomy and diet.) Other members of this group include the bald eagle, the African fish eagle, and the white-tailed sea eagle.

For some fish and sea eagles, the future is uncertain. The striking Steller's sea eagle, which can weigh nearly 20 pounds (9 kg), is believed to have a world population of only about 4,200 breeding pairs. Sanford's sea eagle (*Haliaeetus sanfordi*) and Pallas's sea eagle are also considered to be at risk due to degradation and destruction of their habitat. The total population of the Madagascar fish eagle (*Haliaeetus vociferoides*), believed to be one of the world's rarest birds, is estimated at around forty pairs, which are threatened by both habitat destruction and direct persecution.

Snake or Serpent Eagles

Generally smaller than other eagles, the snake and serpent eagles hunt the savannas and forests of tropical Europe, Asia, Australia, and Africa. The most conspicuous member of this group is the flamboyantly marked bateleur. Its scarlet face and legs stand out boldly against its black, white, and chestnut plumage, and, along with its very short tail, make an adult bateleur unmistakable. The bateleur's name, given by the eighteenth-century French naturalist Le Vaillant, loosely translates as "tumbler" or "tightrope-walker" and undoubtedly

Sea and fish eagles naturally make their homes near water. The view from this particular bald eagle's nest must be spectacular. (Photo © Tom & Pat Leeson)

Eagles of the World

Sea or Fish Eagles

Gypohierax angolensis. Vulturine fish eagle.

Haliaeetus albicilla. White-tailed sea eagle.

Haliaeetus leucogaster. White-bellied sea eagle.

Haliaeetus leucoryphus. Pallas's sea eagle.

Haliaeetus pelagicus. Steller's sea eagle.

Haliaeetus sanfordi. Sanford's fish eagle.

Haliaeetus vocifer. African fish eagle.

Haliaeetus vociferoides. Madagascar fish eagle.

Ichthyophaga humilis. Lesser fish eagle.

Ichthyophaga ichthyaetus. Gray-headed fish eagle.

Snake or Serpent Eagles

Circaetus cinerascens. Banded snake eagle.

Circaetus cinereus. Brown snake eagle.

Circaetus fasciolatus. Fasciated snake eagle.

Circaetus gallicus. Short-toed snake eagle. Includes *C.g. beaudouini*, Beaudouin's snake eagle.

Circaetus pectoralis. Black-chested snake eagle.

Dryotriorchis spectabilis. Congo serpent eagle.

Eutriorchis astur. Madagascar serpent eagle.

Spilornis cheela. Includes *S.c. abbotti*, Simeulue serpent eagle; *S.c. asturinus*, Nias serpent eagle; *S.c. cheela*, Crested serpent eagle; *S.c. natunensis*, Natuna serpent eagle; *S.c. sipora*, Mentawai serpent eagle.

Spilornis elgini. Andaman serpent eagle.

Spilornis holospilus. Philippine serpent eagle. May be a race of *S. cheela*.

Spilornis kinabaluensis. Mountain serpent eagle.

Spilornis minimus. Small serpent eagle. Includes *S.m. klossi*, Nicobar serpent eagle.

Spilornis rufipectus. Sulawesi serpent eagle.

Terathopius ecaudatus. Bateleur.

Booted or True Eagles

Aquila adalberti. Spanish imperial eagle.

Aquila audax. Wedge-tailed eagle.

Aquila chrysaetos. Golden eagle.

Aquila clanga. Greater spotted eagle.

Aquila gurneyi. Gurney's eagle.

Aquila heliaca. Imperial eagle.

Aquila nipalensis. Steppe eagle.

Aquila pomarina. Lesser spotted eagle.

Aquila rapax. African tawny eagle.

Aquila vindhiana. Eurasian tawny eagle.

Aquila wahlbergi. Wahlberg's eagle.

Haliaeetus leucocephalus. Bald eagle.

Hieraaetus ayresii. Ayres's hawk-eagle.

Hieraaetus fasciatus. Bonelli's eagle.

Hieraaetus kienerii. Rufous-bellied eagle.

Hieraaetus morphnoides. Little eagle.

Hieraaetus pennatus. Booted eagle.

Hieraaetus spilogaster. African hawk-eagle.

Ictinaetus malayensis. Black eagle.

Lophoaetus occipitalis. Long-crested eagle.

Oroaetus isidori. Black-and-chestnut eagle.

Polemaetus bellicosus. Martial eagle.

Spizaetus africanus. Cassin's hawk-eagle.

Spizaetus alboniger. Blyth's hawk-eagle.

Spizaetus bartelsi. Javan hawk-eagle.

Spizaetus cirrhatus. Includes *S.c. limnaeetus,* Changeable hawk-eagle; *S.c. cirrhatus,* Crested hawk-eagle; *S.c. floris,* Sunda hawk-eagle.

Spizaetus lanceolatus. Sulawesi hawk-eagle.

Spizaetus nanus. Wallace's hawk-eagle.

Spizaetus nipalensis. Mountain hawk-eagle.

Spizaetus ornatus. Ornate hawk-eagle.

Spizaetus philippensis. Philippine hawk-eagle.

Spizaetus tyrannus. Black hawk-eagle.

Spizastur melanoleucus. Black-and-white hawk-eagle.

Stephanoaetus coronatus. Crowned hawk-eagle.

Harpy or Buteonine Eagles

Harpia harpyja. Harpy eagle.

Harpyhaliaetus coronatus. Crowned eagle.

Harpyhaliaetus solitarius. Solitary eagle.

Harpyopsis novaeguineae. New Guinea eagle.

Morphnus guianensis. Crested eagle.

Pithecophaga jefferyi. Philippine eagle.

The African fish eagle's Latin name, Haliaeetus vocifer, refers to its noisy habit of calling frequently to its mate or to warn other eagles away from its territory. (Photo © Jeremy Woodhouse)

refers to the rocking motion of its flight or the aerobatic maneuvers it sometimes performs.

This group also includes the Madagascar serpent eagle (*Eutriorchis astur*), which is one of the most endangered raptors in the world. For many years, it was doubted whether any survived in the wild. Finally, in 1990, a dead specimen was positively identified, and in 1994, a live Madagascar serpent eagle was caught.

The bird's confirmed presence has added even greater urgency to the ongoing struggle to preserve Madagascar's rain forest habitat upon which so many unique animals depend.

Many of the snake and serpent eagles, particularly those of the genus *Spilornis*, have a very restricted range, which may be limited to one group of islands. This means that any destruction or degradation of their habitat poses a critical threat to their survival.

The most widespread eagle in the world, the golden eagle is also one of the most persecuted. (Photo © W. Perry Conway)

Booted or True Eagles

The booted eagles get their name because their legs are feathered right down to their ankles. This group contains the most species and numbers among them some of the most beautifully marked eagles, including the ornate hawk-eagle (*Spizaetus ornatus*), the Spanish imperial eagle (*Aquila adalberti*), and the crowned hawk-eagle. Several eagles in this group sport dashing, long crest feathers. Some booted eagles, including the martial eagle, the wedge-tailed eagle (*Aquila audax*), and Verreaux's eagle, are among the largest eagles in the world; others, such as Wahlberg's eagle (*Aquila wahlbergi*) and Ayres's hawk-eagle, are some of the smallest. The crowned hawk-eagle has been described as one of the most powerful eagles on earth and regularly eats mammals up to twice its weight.

Two booted eagles, the golden eagle and the wedge-tailed eagle, were persecuted mercilessly in the past for their supposed habits as stock killers. Today, other members of the group are facing even greater threats. Wallace's hawk-eagle (*Spizaetus nanus*), the Philippine hawk-eagle (*Spizaetus philippensis*), and the imperial eagle (*Aquila heliaca*) are considered to be highly at risk; the Javan hawk-eagle (*Spizaetus bartelsi*)

The magnificent Verreaux's eagle is best known for its intricate courtship flights, filled with aerobatics. These eagles prefer to nest near colonies of hyraxes, their favorite prey. (Photo © HPH Photography/Bruce Coleman)

and the Spanish imperial eagle are in even more extreme peril. Deforestation of its home, combined with pressure from illegal hunting and capture for profit, has left the Javan hawk-eagle facing a bleak future. In contrast, it was reforestation, replacement of its native forest habitat with more commercially valuable trees, that was a major factor in reducing the remaining world population of Spanish imperial eagles to only about 150 pairs. Unlike the new eucalyptus and pine plantations, the original ancient oak forest was rabbit-rich and largely left alone by humans.

The vulnerability of one of the Spanish imperial eagles' last remaining refuges, Doñana National Park, was evident in April 1998 when toxic mining sludge spilled into the park's Guadiamar River, resulting in massive deaths of fish and invertebrates. Observers worried that the dead animals would be eaten by others in the park, including the eagles, spreading the disaster even farther. The final ecological toll will remain unknown for some time. Doñana's fragile offer of sanctuary is also threatened by the power lines surrounding the park. Researchers have determined that electrocution is the main cause of mortality among the park's eagle population, and that the victims are mainly juvenile females, whose survival is critical for the recovery of the species. Their larger size means that females are more likely than males to make a fatal connection, touching a live wire while perched on a metal supporting pylon. Burying transmission lines could eliminate this hazard but it is an expensive solution. Another drain on the species is the significant number of Spanish imperial eagle chicks that die each year due to Cainism. Removing chicks to foster nests is helping to reduce these losses.

Harpy or Buteonine Eagles

At home in the tropical forests of South America, Mexico, New Guinea, and the Philippines, this group of six contains some of the world's most magnificent eagles, including the harpy eagle, the New Guinea eagle (*Harpyopsis novaeguineae*), and the Philippine eagle (*Pithecophaga jefferyi*).

Although other eagles are almost as heavy and some have larger wingspans, the harpy eagle of South America is without doubt the world's most powerful eagle. A female harpy eagle may weigh nearly 20 pounds (9 kg). Her legs may be as big around as a child's wrist; her feet tipped with 1.5-inch-long (3.75-cm-long) talons may span 9 inches (22.5 cm). With those legs and talons, the harpy is able to snatch large arboreal prey, including sloths and howler monkeys, from the branches where they live. It required slow-motion footage shot in Guyana to reveal the technique employed by the harpy to take a sloth hanging from a branch. Deftly rolling in flight to pass under the branch, the eagle grabbed the sloth, wrenched it loose, and carried it off with hardly a break in its flight. A harpy eagle swooping down at 20 miles per hour (32 kph) generates approximately 13,500 foot-pounds (18,300 Newton-meters) of energy—that's more than twice the muzzle energy of a bullet shot from a heavy rifle. Recent research has indicated that even the harpy eagle cannot carry the biggest animals it kills back to its nest. Adult harpy eagles probably feed on a carcass for a day or two before they eventually carry the more manageable maggoty remains to their chicks.

Bateleurs regularly fly hundreds of miles a day over the African savanna in their search for prey. This young bird has not yet developed the brightly colored plumage that will make it so conspicuous as an adult. (Photo © Jeremy Woodhouse)

On the other side of the world, soaring above the beech forests of lower mountain slopes, the New Guinea eagle searches for prey that may include wallabies, piglets, and tree kangaroos. New Guinea highlanders still hunt this eagle for its wing and tail feathers, which they use in headdresses. Sadly, this practice along with the continuing destruction of its habitat means that the age-old sight of a hunting New Guinea eagle may be denied to future generations.

The stunning Philippine eagle, until recently known as the monkey-eating eagle, apparently eats more flying lemurs than monkeys. (These lemurs are 2-foot/ 60-cm-long nocturnal mammals, not Madagascar primates.) There probably never were a great number of Philippine eagles: One estimate puts the maximum historical population at around six thousand individuals. As the Philippine Islands became more populated and the forests were stripped from the land, the eagle lost its home and hunting territory, and became vulnerable to shooting and trapping. Although valiant efforts to save the species continue, for the Philippine eagle, time is running out: Fewer than two hundred Philippine eagles remain, and the old-growth forest they need to survive continues to be destroyed.

Two of the best-known species of eagles, and two that show both the depredation wrought by humans on eagle populations and the extent to which repopulation efforts can succeed, are the golden and bald eagles.

With feathers running right down to its "ankles," this long-crested eagle is one of the booted eagles. (Photo © Stan Osolinski)

Golden Eagle

Catch sight of a golden eagle in flight, its feathers gilded by the sun's rays, and it is easy to understand why so many different peoples chose this bird as a symbol of strength and power. Perhaps the most wide-spread bird of its size in the world, the golden eagle soars on 7-foot (2.1-m) wings over much of the Northern Hemisphere. It prefers the rugged terrain of mountainous areas and prairie coulees, places where the rough land causes an abundance of updrafts. Here the golden eagle hunts for a wide variety of prey, often hare and rabbit, but also animals such as waterfowl, grouse, carrion, ground squirrels, and other assorted small mammals.

When they are about four or five years old, golden eagles choose their mates, and they often keep the same partners for their entire fifteen- to twenty-year lives. Golden eagles usually build their large nests on rocky cliffs and ledges, but they will also nest in trees. A mated pair may return to the same territory year after year, sometimes alternating between more than one aerie within that territory. After adding fresh material to that season's chosen nest, the eagles settle in to brood their one to three eggs, which hatch into pale gray, downy chicks after about six weeks. Golden eagles are one of the species in which Cain and Abel behavior is seen, and so, although more than one chick may hatch, sometimes only one survives. The young golden eagles are ready to attempt their first flights about seventy days after hatching.

Riders of many winds, golden eagles demonstrate superbly controlled flight in a wide variety of conditions. Leslie Brown watched golden eagles in Scotland soar effortlessly on days when there was hardly a whisper of air movement and, on another occasion, appear to hang rock steady in winds that were strong enough to tear slabs of turf from the nearby cliff face. During their courtship flights, golden eagles rocket earthward with their wings folded, sometimes reaching an estimated 100 miles per hour (160 km/h) only to swing upward once more. Or the two eagles may shoot past one another, briefly touching talons. These exuberant displays may also be performed by small groups of eagles, providing a spectacular air show for the observer fortunate enough to see them. The purpose of these golden eagle gatherings is not known, but many who have watched in fascination write that the eagles seem to be flying for the sheer joy of it.

A golden eagle lifts itself into the sky—a killing field not long ago but now a place of safety. (Photo © W. Perry Conway)

Despite their status as powerful symbols for many cultures, golden eagles have suffered greatly from human persecution. Near the end of the eighteenth century, European gamekeepers and sheep farmers began the slaughter using guns, traps, and poisoned bait. As sport-hunting pressure increased, gamekeepers viewed eagles, and other birds of prey, as unwelcome competitors for valuable game that rightfully belonged in the hunter's bag. The scale of the persecution due to this attitude became evident during the two world wars when, with gamekeepers busy elsewhere, raptor populations began to climb.

Golden eagles need space and wilderness to survive. (Photo © W. Perry Conway)

Sheep farmers have long believed that eagles dine heavily on mutton and lamb. Although isolated incidents of heavy predation by individual eagles have been observed, modern studies reveal that golden eagles usually take only dead or dying sheep, and that eagles play a negligible role in total sheep mortality. Indeed, golden eagles actually help sheep farmers by killing large numbers of rabbits and ground squirrels that compete with sheep for forage. Although a few farmers realized this and allowed eagles to remain on their land, for most farmers with sheep the only good eagle was a dead eagle.

In the southern United States, between 1950 and 1970, gunners in airplanes were paid to shoot eagles. An estimated twenty thousand eagles were killed. The victims were mostly golden eagles but bald eagles were also shot. Many of the dead eagles were wintering visitors, meaning that the slaughter affected eagle populations over a far greater area than that in which the actual killing took place. Much of this butchery was financed by sheep ranchers, who added to the death toll by placing poison baits that were

Golden eagles have a special place in the mythology of many peoples. They were often considered messengers of the gods. (Photo © Lynn Stone)

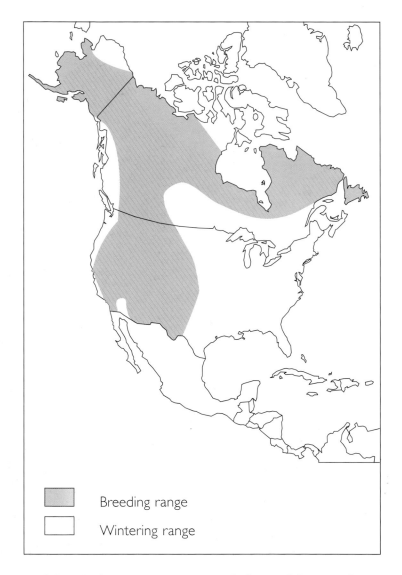

Breeding range

Wintering range

North American range of the golden eagle

Downy and still helpless, two four-week-old golden eagles wait for food in their cliffside aerie. (Photo © W. Perry Conway)

intended for coyotes but also killed eagles as a grisly bonus. The federal government, through the Department of the Interior's Division of Wildlife Services (later known as Animal Damage Control), also played its part in the tragedy by putting out its own non-specific poison baits, despite the common knowledge that eagles were being killed by accident. The shooting and poisoning continued even after the eagles received legal protection in 1940 (bald eagles) and 1962 (golden eagles).

Killing eagles for cash is distasteful enough, but many hunters shot eagles from planes not for money but for fun. Contemporary magazine and newspaper articles gave breathless first-person accounts of the challenging and exciting new sport, encouraging others to give it a try. These assaults on common sense were not allowed to go unchallenged—the stories were usually swiftly followed by passionately outraged editorials from a variety of sources. The defense of eagles grew to be a popular cause and was one of the first strong indications that attitudes about animals, particularly predators, were beginning to change.

The golden eagle's diet proved to be its best defense against another major threat—pesticides. The small grass-eating rodents that make up the majority of a golden eagle's food do not ingest and concentrate pesticide residues in the same lethal amounts as fish and waterfowl. Because of this, unlike many other raptors, golden eagles largely escaped the consequences of heavy pesticide use in the post-war years.

The golden eagle was the bird of Zeus and the standard of the Roman legions. Golden eagles were adopted as the symbol of rebirth in baptism by the early Christians and still serve as messengers to the Hopi gods. Today we have debunked the myth of the golden eagle as stock killer and have developed an understanding of how predators fit into healthy ecosystems: We are learning to value intangibles such as the sheer beauty of a golden eagle against a deep blue prairie sky. Current golden eagle populations are, in general, stable and healthy. We can help to keep them that way by preserving the lands that the golden eagle, soaring symbol of wild places, needs for the future.

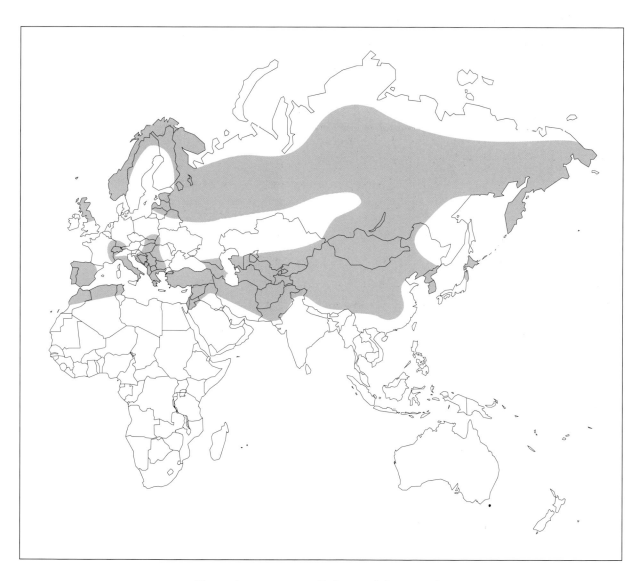

Eurasian range of the golden eagle

Bald Eagle

With its gleaming white head and tail, an adult bald eagle can be mistaken for no other bird. Bald eagles also have the distinction of being the sole eagle species unique to North America. Dining mainly on fish, but also eating other foods—including ducks, snakes, rodents, and carrion—bald eagles grow to be large birds. A male may weigh 7 to 10 pounds (3.2–4.6 kg) and have a wingspan of about 6.5 feet (2 m). The larger female may weigh as much as 14 pounds (6.4 kg) and have a wingspan of up to 8 feet (2.4 m). In the wild, bald eagles may live to be thirty years old, although most do not survive this long.

Those distinctive head and tail feathers do not appear until bald eagles reach maturity at four to five years of age. At about this time, bald eagles select their mates, which they are believed to keep for life. Each year in the early spring, the pair constructs or, more commonly, refurbishes a nest, which is usually in a treetop near a source of water. Bald eagle aeries are often used over a span of many years, sometimes by more than one generation of eagles, with each nesting season bringing the addition of fresh material by the current tenants. Like the famous Vermilion, Ohio, aerie described earlier, some bald eagle nests become very large. After only fifteen years of annual occupation, a nearly cylindrical nest in Pennsylvania measured 9 feet (2.7 m) tall with a diameter of 6 feet (1.8 m).

Into a shallow depression atop this magnificent receptacle, the female bald eagle lays her eggs, usually two or three, which hatch after about thirty-five days into down-covered, helpless chicks. Fed with great care by attentive parents, the 3-ounce (85-g) chicks grow rapidly, and in about three months are ready for their first flights. By the time they are about four months old, the bald eaglets are ready to face the hazards of life on their own—and the perils are many.

In 1782, the fledgling United States of America chose the then-common bald eagle as the country's national symbol over the protests of some who, like Benjamin Franklin, felt the bird was disreputable and unworthy of such an honor. (Franklin objected to the bald eagle's often-observed technique of stealing an osprey's catch rather than doing its own fishing. He felt that this showed a decided lack of moral character on the eagle's part.) Wildlife experts estimate that at this time there were between 25,000 and 75,000

A bald eagle perched near the shoreline is an unmistakeable, and unforgettable, sight. (Photo © Henry H. Holdsworth)

Like other eagles, bald eagles are good parents who provide food, warmth, and shelter to their helpless chicks. (Photo © Henry H. Holdsworth

bald eagles nesting in the lower forty-eight states. One hundred and eighty years later, in the early 1960s, the nesting population of bald eagles in this same area had plummeted to fewer than 450 pairs, and the bald eagle was in danger of extinction throughout most of its range. There were several reasons for the dramatic decline.

To prosper, bald eagles need mature trees in which to nest and a peaceful place to raise their young. As humans established and expanded settlements, nesting trees were cut down or made unsuitable because of increased noise and activity in the area. Gradually, relentlessly, bald eagles were forced to give way before "progress." This process was accelerated because bald eagles, and other raptors, were viewed as stock killers that preyed on lambs and chickens. Thousands of eagles were slaughtered with gun and poison. Still more eagles were shot by sport hunters, and for some time, it was considered chic to have a stuffed bald eagle to display. Finally taking note of the decline of the national symbol, the U.S. Congress passed the Bald Eagle Protection Act in 1940, making it illegal to kill, harass, possess (without a permit), or sell bald eagles.

The Bald Eagle Protection Act did not apply in Alaska, however, where, between 1917 and 1953, more than 100,000 bald eagles were killed for bounty at the instigation of fur farmers and salmon fishers. Fur farmers were angry that bald eagles sometimes ate fox pups. The eagles did this because Arctic foxes had been dumped on islands with nesting seabird colonies, which were intended to provide the foxes with "free" food. The foxes de-

Captive-raised bald eaglets that will later be released into the wild are often fed by a concealed human using an eagle puppet. This keeps the eaglets from associating people with food, a habit that could be fatal in later life. (Photo © Frank Oberle)

voured the birds, and deprived of their natural prey, the bald eagles nesting in the vicinity began to feed fox pups to their chicks. Salmon fishers blamed bald eagles for declining catches, even though the eagles preferred dead and dying post-spawning fish. As several observers pointed out, until the advent of heavy commercial fishing, there had always been more than enough salmon for eagles, gulls, bears, and humans.

By the end of the bounty period, a pair of talons brought the eagle killer the whopping sum of U.S.$2.00. The slaughter finally ended in 1953, but by that time a much bigger threat to the bald eagle was already beginning to make its effects felt.

Following World War II, there was a great movement to take advantage of recently discovered wonder chemicals. Among these were a group of pesticides known as organochlorines, whose most well-known member is DDT. Widely used and often applied aerially over large areas, DDT and its relatives washed down into streams, rivers, lakes, and estuaries, then made their way into the aquatic food chain. Concentrated in the fatty tissues of fish, the toxic residues were unwittingly transported to eagle aeries by parents bringing food to their young. Here, the chemicals sometimes caused the death of the young or parent birds directly, or weakened them so that they were unable to stave off other attacks on their systems. More insidiously, these chemicals caused female eagles to lay eggs with shells too fragile to survive brooding. As the effects of DDT became apparent, a widespread outcry began, heralded by Rachel Carson's famous book *Silent Spring* (1962). It took until 1972 for the United States to ban the chemical for most applications, and it is still freely used in some countries today. Yet another chemical threat came from a more low-tech source—lead shot. Bald eagles eating dead or hunter-crippled waterfowl could ingest enough lead shot to suffer from fatal lead-poisoning. To combat this problem, as of 1997, lead shot was banned for use in hunting waterfowl in both the United States and Canada.

Beginning in 1976 and continuing well into the 1990s, several efforts were made to reintroduce bald eagles into parts of their former range that were clean enough to support them. Some of the birds were captive-bred, but most were raised from eggs or chicks collected in the wild. After a few false starts, the newly introduced birds began to breed, and wild eagle populations began to recover. Perhaps the best indicator of the bald eagle's progress was its official down-listing in 1995 from "endangered" to "threatened." However, the bald eagle's continued existence is by no means assured, and we must not allow that fact that it no longer bears the eye-catching "endangered" designation to lull us into a false sense of security. What we should learn from the bald eagle's recovery is that with careful thought, determination, and a great deal of effort, humans can help species that are in trouble, and we can avoid the same problems in the future. Perched regally in a tree near the shore of a northern lake, its white head drawing the eye like a beacon, the bald eagle reminds us of what is possible when we care enough.

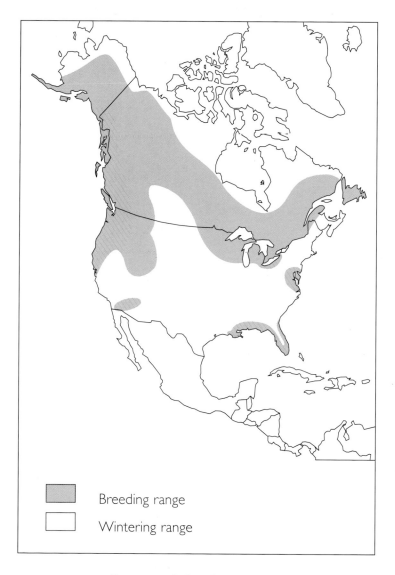

Breeding range

Wintering range

Range of the Bald Eagle

*The bald eagle's appetite for fish put it on Alaskan salmon fishermen's
"most wanted" list from 1917 to 1953, resulting in the killing of more than
100,000 birds. (Photo © Michael H. Francis)*

This young bald eagle displays the mottled plumage of an immature bird. Bald eagles do not get their signature white head and tail until they are about four or five years old. (Photo © Frank Oberle)

Eagles and Humans

Early peoples respected eagles for the powers they believed the eagles possessed. Because of their ability to soar into the heavens, in many cultures, eagles were linked to the sun, the gods, and the journey of souls. Eagle feathers, bones, and claws all had talismanic powers and were associated with important rituals, such as the Eagle Dance of the Comanches and the Sun Dance of the Lakota in North America. Some cultures made these great birds even larger, transforming them into the legendary Thunderbird of the Pacific Northwest or the Roc of the Middle East. Tales of human encounters with eagles almost always portrayed the eagles as wise and powerful, often giving gifts to worthy individuals.

To our ancestors, the world was a place where humans and animals were both parts of a whole, each playing their part, and each dependent on the other. As people settled in communities and on farms, this belief began to change. People in towns and cities became detached from wild lands and wild animals, retaining only the symbolic view of eagles without an appreciation for the bird itself. To the farmers, still in touch with the land, existence at subsistence levels meant the formerly admirable hunting skills of eagles were now perceived as a threat to valuable livestock. The lamb-snatching, goat-kid-killing eagle became firmly entrenched in folk wisdom. Old beliefs became inverted. Where once the eagle had been seen as creator of humans and carrier of new souls to this world, dark tales now told of rapacious eagles carrying off children. (Incidentally, no documented cases of this feat exist, and experiments indicate that the lifting power of most eagles would be inadequate for all but the youngest infants.)

Slowly, a new environmental awareness began to creep over the world in the 1960s and 1970s. Eagles became symbols of the wilderness and of all that we had inflicted upon it. More and more people developed an interest in the great birds for themselves as well as for their symbolic value. In 1990, a brief magazine article revealed how much things had changed. The story noted that, with little to do since the collapse of the Berlin Wall, German border guards were now protecting eagle nests in the former "death strip" between East and West Germany. The fact that the nests needed protection at all makes it clear that our journey toward awareness has just begun.

It is easy to understand how, looking up at a sight like this, ancient peoples could talk of cities above where "Eagle People" lived. (Photo © W. Perry Conway)

An immature bald eagle rides the winds. (Photo © Michael H. Francis)

This bald eagle appears to be attempting to ignore its raucous companion. (Photo © Thomas D. Mangelsen)

The Future

What does the future hold for eagles or, more pointedly, is there to be a future for them at all? Our past actions have placed eagles in an extremely perilous position. Without question, it will take our present and future intervention to give eagles a chance for survival. The bald eagle's comeback has shown us what can be accomplished, and intensive efforts are under way to help other species, including the Philippine eagle and the eagles of Madagascar.

Despite protective legislation, people continue to kill eagles deliberately. Increasing both preventative education and punitive measures could reduce this problem. Getting local people involved in eagle conservation has proved to be highly effective in places like Venezuela, where a logging crew that had been informed about eagles stopped cutting when they spied a nesting harpy eagle. The crew adopted and watched over the nest, allowing the eagle to raise its chick to maturity.

Reducing unintentional eagle deaths is also important. For example, wind turbines in California, highly touted as a "green" energy source, kill a number of eagles and other raptors each year—five hundred birds of prey during one two-year study. The turbines and the eagles will continue to occupy the same areas because they are dependent on the same resource—wind. Design modifications could help to reduce the death toll. By examining technology in the light of values that include the needs of all species, we can make decisions that are beneficial for humans as well as animals.

By far the greatest threat to eagles, and to all wildlife, is habitat destruction. Those eagle species that are currently holding their own must be protected from land development that could tip the scales against them. As for eagles species already in trouble, there is simply no alternative to habitat protection. Rapidly advancing reproductive technology allows us to use extraordinary means to preserve species.

We have identified eagles with gods and endowed them with supernatural powers. We have drawn upon the magic in an eagle's feather. Ever since humans first gazed in wonder at a soaring eagle, we have linked the concepts of freedom and strength to the spirit of these great birds. We must now use our strength to ensure there will be eagles flying free in the skies of our future.

The recovery of the bald eagle provides the voice of hope for all eagles. With similar concentrated efforts, we may be able to save even some of the most endangered species. (Photo © W. Perry Conway)

Information gained through the efforts of dedicated amateurs, like this eagle bander, has helped to provide a basis for making decisions that consider the needs of eagles and other species. (Photo © Glen & Rebecca Grambo)

As a symbol for the United States, the bald eagle has become instantly recognizable to people who live far from the bird's territory. (Photo © Henry H. Holdsworth)

Index

Accipitridae, 9

African fish eagle (*Haliaeetus vocifer*), 27, 38, 39, 40

Ayres's hawk-eagle (*Hieraaetus ayresii*), 11, 19, 39, 41

bald eagle (*Haliaeetus leucocephalus*), 39, 44, 55–61
   diet, 19, 24, 55, 57
   physical characteristics, 17
   range, 24, 59
   reintroduction, 58

Bald Eagle Protection Act, 57

banded snake eagle, 30, 38

bateleur (*Terathopius ecaudatus*), 15, 37, 38, 44

beaks, 15

Benjamin Franklin, 55

black eagle (*Ictinaetus malayensis*), 12, 39

Bonelli's eagle (*Hieraaetus fasciatus*), 19, 39

bones, 15, 17

booted or true eagles, 39, 41–43

Brown, Leslie, 9, 20

Cain and Abel behavior (Cainism), 32, 35, 43, 47

Carson, Rachel, 58

Cathartidae, 9

Comanches, 63

communication, 27, 40

conservation efforts, 35, 43, 57, 58

courtship, 27, 30, 47

crowned hawk-eagle (*Stephanoaetus coronatus*), 12, 15, 27, 39, 41

DDT, 58

diet, 12, 15, 19–21, 23-24, 32, 43–44, 47

Eagle Dance, 63

"eagle," definition of, 9

eagles, in legend and myth, 7, 52, 63, 67

eaglets, 32, 35, 55

eggs, 32, 58

eyes, 11–12

Falconiformes, 9

Falconidae, 9

feathers, 15, 17, 35

fish eagles, see sea or fish eagles

flight, 14, 15, 17, 19, 23, 24, 27, 35

Gargett, Valerie, 32, 35

golden eagle (*Aquila chrysaetos*), 44, 47–53
   diet, 19, 39, 47, 52
   in legend and myth, 49, 52
   range, 41, 47, 50, 53

gray-headed fish eagle (*Ichthyophaga ichthyaetus*), 14, 38

habitat destruction, 37, 41, 43, 44, 57, 67

harpy eagle (*Harpia harpyja*), 11, 27, 39, 43

harpy or buteonine eagles, 15, 43

hawk-eagle (*Spizaetus ornatus*), 41

imperial eagle (*Aquila heliaca*), 41

Javan hawk-eagle (*Spizaetus bartelsi*), 39, 41, 43

Lakota, 63

lesser fish eagle (*Ichthyophaga humilis*), 12, 38

lesser spotted eagle (*Aquila pomarina*), 19, 23, 35, 39

little eagle (*Hieraaetus morphnoides*), 11, 39

long-crested eagle (*Lophoaetus occipitalis*), 23, 39, 45

Madagascar fish eagle (*Haliaeetus vociferoides*), 37, 38, 67

Madagascar serpent eagle (*Eutriorchis astur*), 38, 41, 67

martial eagle (*Polemaetus bellicosus*), 12, 15, 39, 41

mating, 27, 30, 35, 47

migration, 24

nest, 27, 29–30, 35, 47, 55

New Guinea eagle (*Harpyopsis novaeguineae*), 39, 43, 44

Nias serpent eagle (*Spilornis cheela asturinus*), 11, 38

origins, 9

Pallas' sea eagle (*Haliaeetus leucoryphus*), 20, 37, 38

Pandionidae, 9

Philippine eagle (*Pithecophaga*

jefferyi), 11, 39, 43, 44, 67

Philippine hawk-eagle (*Spizaetus philippensis*), 39, 41

Roc, 63

Saggitaridae, 9

Sanford's sea eagle (*Haliaeetus sanfordi*), 37, 38

sea or fish eagles, 12, 15, 20, 37, 38

sexual dimorphism, 11

snake or serpent eagles, 11, 15, 20, 23, 37, 38, 41

Spanish imperial eagle (*Aquila adalberti*), 39, 41, 43

Steller's sea eagle (*Haliaeetus pelagicus*), 15, 19, 20, 37, 38

steppe eagle (*Aquila nipalensis*), 20, 23, 39

Sun Dance, 63

talons, 12, 15, 43

taxonomy, 9, 38–39

tawny eagle (*Aquila rapax*), 20

territory, 21, 27

thermals, 23, 24

Thunderbird, 63

Verreaux's eagle (*Aquila verreauxii*), 23, 41, 42

vision, 11–12

vulturine fish eagle (*Gypohierax angolensis*), 23, 38

Wahlberg's eagle (*Aquila wahlbergi*), 39, 41

Wallace's hawk-eagle (*Spizaetus nanus*), 39, 41

wedge-tailed eagle (*Aquila audax*), 19, 39, 41

weight, 11, 17, 37, 43, 55

white-bellied sea eagle (*Haliaeetus leucogaster*), 20

white-tailed sea eagle (*Haliaeetus albicilla*), 20, 38

wings, 11, 12, 14, 15, 17, 35, 43

Recommended Reading

For more information about eagles, try the following books:

Brown, Leslie. Any of his many books—he spent a lifetime studying these great birds.

Gerrard, Jon M., and Gary R. Bortolotti. *The Bald Eagle: Haunts and Habits of a Wilderness Monarch*. Washington: Smithsonian Institution Press, 1988; Saskatoon, Sask.: Western Producer Prairie Books, 1988. A detailed look at the fortunes of North America's most familiar eagle.

Grambo, Rebecca L. *Eagles: Masters of the Sky*. Stillwater, MN: Voyageur Press, 1997. A celebration of the world's eagles through an anthology of poetry, natural history, art, and folklore.

Olendorff, Richard R. *Golden Eagle Country*. New York: Knopf, 1975. A wonderful account of North America's "other" eagle.

Tuchman, Gail. *Through the Eye of the Feather: Native American Visions*. Layton, Utah: Gibbs Smith, 1994. This book is helpful in understanding the eagle's place in Native American traditions.

About the Author

Rebecca L. Grambo is a natural history writer and outdoor photographer who has always had a love for animals and an insatiable curiosity about their lives. She lives in Warman, Saskatchewan, with her husband, Glen. She is also the author of *Eagles: Masters of the Sky* (Voyageur Press), *The World of the Fox*, *Mountain Lion*, and several children's books. (Photo © Glen and Rebecca Grambo)